Zoo

By Jennifer Colby

Published in the United States of America by
Cherry Lake Publishing
Ann Arbor, Michigan
www.cherrylakepublishing.com

Content Adviser: Dr. Sharon L. Deem
Reading Adviser: Marla Conn MS, Ed., Literacy specialist, Read-Ability, Inc.

Photo Credits: © Nadezhda1906/Shutterstock Images, cover, 1; © YC_Chee/Shutterstock Images, 4; © belizar/Shutterstock Images, 6; © JaySi/Shutterstock Images, 8; © Marina99/Shutterstock Images, 10; © Bork/Shutterstock Images, 12; © beltsazar/Shutterstock Images, 14; © Rob Hainer/Shutterstock Images, 16; © Monkey Business Images/Shutterstock Images, 18; © pistolseven/Shutterstock Images, 20

Copyright © 2017 by Cherry Lake Publishing
All rights reserved. No part of this book may be reproduced or utilized in any form or by any means without written permission from the publisher.

Library of Congress Cataloging-in-Publication Data
Names: Colby, Jennifer, 1971- author.
Title: Zoo / by Jennifer Colby.
Description: Ann Arbor : Cherry Lake Publishing, [2016] | Series: 21st
 century junior library. Explore a workplace | Audience: K to grade 3.
Identifiers: LCCN 2015048713| ISBN 9781634710800 (hardcover) | ISBN 9781634712781 (pbk.) | ISBN 9781634711791 (pdf) | ISBN 9781634713771 (ebook)
Subjects: LCSH: Zoos—Juvenile literature. | Zoos—Employees—Juvenile
 literature. | Zoos—Vocational guidance—Juvenile literature.
Classification: LCC QL76 .C635 2016 | DDC 590.73—dc23
LC record available at http://lccn.loc.gov/2015048713

Cherry Lake Publishing would like to acknowledge the work of The Partnership for 21st Century Learning. Please visit *www.p21.org* for more information.

Printed in the United States of America
Corporate Graphics

CONTENTS

5   What Is a Zoo?

9   Zoo Workers

19 Do You Want to Work at a Zoo?

22 Glossary
23 Find Out More
24 Index
24 About the Author

Zoo workers give chimps many things to climb on.

What Is a Zoo?

Look over there! It's an elephant. Look at its big ears. Do you see the penguins? They are swimming in the water. Maybe you are watching the **chimpanzees** swing around their **enclosure**. Welcome to the zoo!

Zoo workers feed the animals.

Zoos are all over the world. Have you been to a zoo? You can see many kinds of animals at a zoo.

People work at zoos. They help visitors learn and have fun. Zoo workers must keep the animals healthy and safe.

It is fun to see the zoo animals up close!

Zoo Workers

You see many animals when you visit the zoo. However, you may not see all the zoo workers. Many of them work in areas that are closed to zoo visitors.

Ask Questions!

Which animals need the most care? Which animals need more space? What animal has lived there a long time? Do you have questions? Ask a zoo worker. You may learn something new about zoos!

Zoos must provide proper care and housing to many different kinds of animals.

The zoo **director** is in charge of the zoo. A zoo director must supervise the zoo staff, raise money for the zoo, and make sure the zoo runs properly.

Each animal needs its own special care. Each animal needs different types of spaces. The director makes sure the zoo has the proper employees and resources to keep the animals happy and healthy.

When animals get sick, veterinarians give them medicine.

12

Zookeepers take care of the animals. They give the animals fresh food and water. They clean their enclosures. They watch the animals.

Zookeepers notice when an animal is not right. They ask the **veterinarian** for help if an animal looks sick. Veterinarians work hard to make sure the animals stay healthy.

Think!

Would you like to be a zookeeper? You will need to know a lot about animals. What classes should you take in high school and college? Most zookeepers study **biology** and **zoology**.

Maintenance crews keep zoos looking good.

A **maintenance crew** makes sure the zoo looks tidy and clean. Workers fix things that are broken. **Gardeners** trim bushes and trees. They also pull weeds and water plants. The maintenance crew works together to keep the zoo clean and safe for animals and human visitors.

Look!

Look around the next time you are at the zoo. Do you see a lot of plants? Plants help keep the animals happy and comfortable. Different animals like different plants. Why do you think that is?

A ticket booth worker sells you a ticket to the zoo.

Not all workers at the zoo work with animals. Some workers help people who come to the zoo.

You might need a ticket to enter the zoo. Workers collect your money at the ticket booth. Other people work in the gift shop. Some workers might sell you food in a snack bar.

Taking care of a pet is a fun way to learn about animals.

Do You Want to Work at a Zoo?

Would you like to work at a zoo? You can start getting ready now.

Do you have a pet? Taking care of a pet is a great way to get started. Maybe you do not have a pet. Ask if you can take care of a friend's pet.

It takes many people to run a zoo.

If you want to work at a zoo, learn as much as you can about animals. A nearby zoo might have programs you can go to. Books and Web sites can teach you about animals. You can also learn from online nature videos. Maybe one day you will work at the zoo!

GLOSSARY

biology (bye-AH-luh-jee) the study of living things

chimpanzees (chim-pan-ZEEZ) a type of great ape that comes from Africa; also called chimps

director (duh-REK-tur) the head of an organization such as a zoo

enclosure (en-KLOH-zhur) a closed-off area where animals live

gardeners (GAHR-duhn-urz) people who take care of plants

maintenance crew (MAYN-tuh-nuhns KROO) a group of workers who take care of a zoo's buildings, outdoor areas, and equipment

veterinarian (vet-ur-uh-NAIR-ee-uhn) a doctor trained to provide health care to all kinds of animals

zookeepers (ZOO-kee-purz) people in charge of a zoo's animals

zoology (zoh-AH-luh-jee) the scientific study of animals

FIND OUT MORE

BOOKS

Hestermann, Josh, and Bethanie Hestermann. *Zoology for Kids: Understanding and Working with Animals*. Chicago: Chicago Review Press, 2015.

Shaw, Gina. *Curious About Zoo Vets*. New York: Grosset & Dunlap, 2015.

WEB SITES

Saint Louis Zoo—So You Want to Be a Zookeeper?
www.stlzoo.org/animals/soyouwanttobeazookeeper/
Learn how to become a zookeeper.

San Diego Zoo Kids—Jobs at the Zoo: Zoo Keeper
http://kids.sandiegozoo.org/jobs-zoo/zoo-keeper
Take a look at one of the jobs that makes the zoo run.

INDEX

B
biology, 13
books, 21

C
chimpanzees, 5
cleaning, 13, 15

D
directors, 11

E
elephants, 5
enclosures, 5, 13

F
food, 13, 17

G
gardeners, 15
gift shops, 17

H
health, 7, 11, 13

M
maintenance crews, 15

P
penguins, 5
pets, 19
plants, 15
programs, 21

Q
questions, 9

S
safety, 7, 15
snack bars, 17

T
tickets, 17

V
veterinarians, 13
videos, 21
visitors, 7, 9, 15

W
water, 5, 13, 15
Web sites, 21
workers, 7, 9, 15, 17

Z
zookeepers, 13
zoology, 13

ABOUT THE AUTHOR

Jennifer Colby is the author of many books for children. She is a high school librarian. She likes to go with her children to Binder Park Zoo in Battle Creek, Michigan.